It's Me, Zoey!

Written by
Alexis Hale

Illustrated by
Jason Lam

Hello!

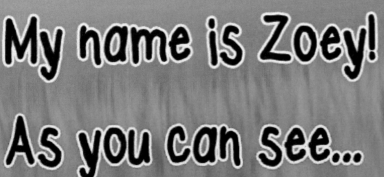

My name is Zoey!

As you can see...

I'm a little different
but I'm totally me!

I can do it all.

Just give me a chance.

"I don't know!" I tell them.

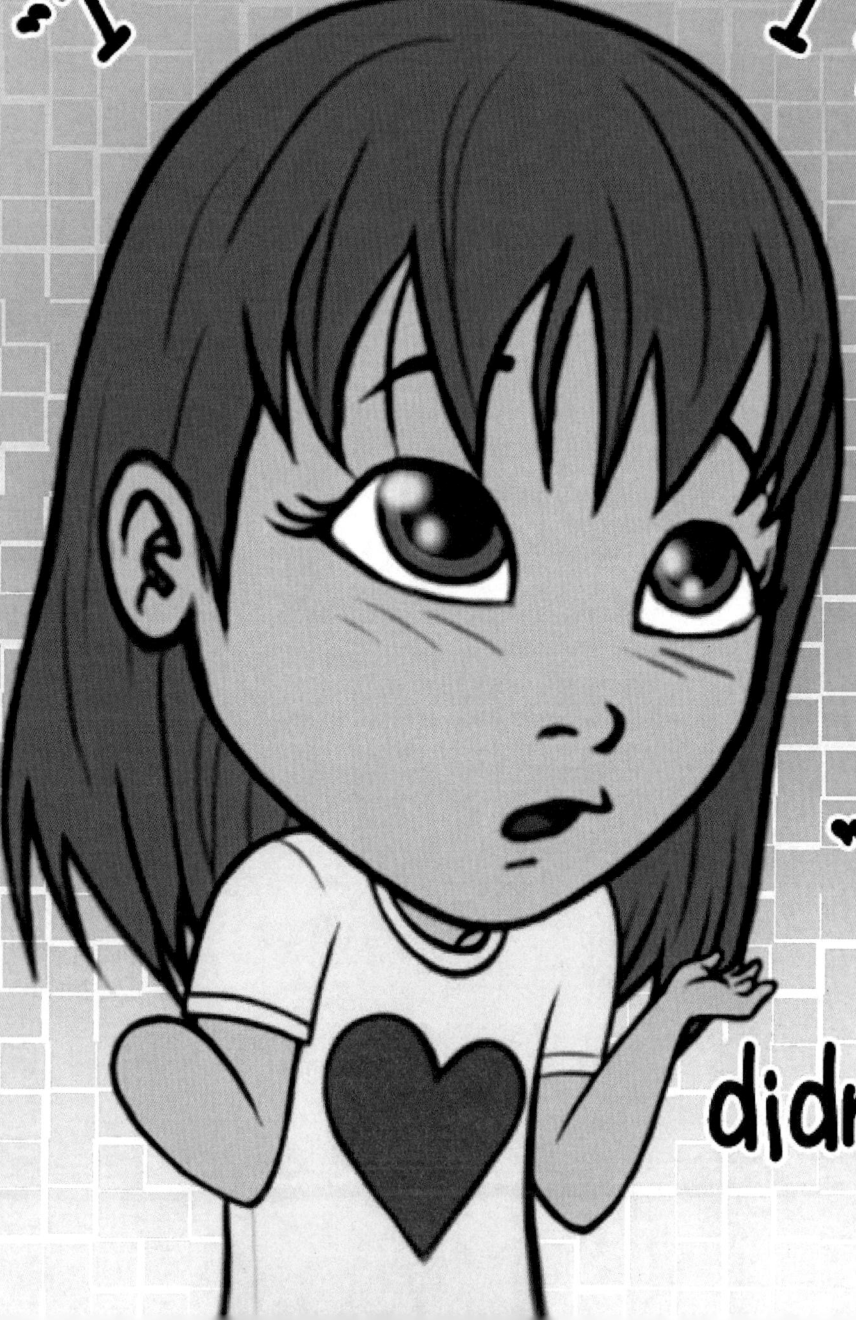

"It just didn't grow."

We are all unique
in our own way.

Kim's hair is purple and Sparkles in the sun.

Tyler is tall and strong.

He looks out for me.

Samantha is the calm to all of my CRAZY.

We are all different.

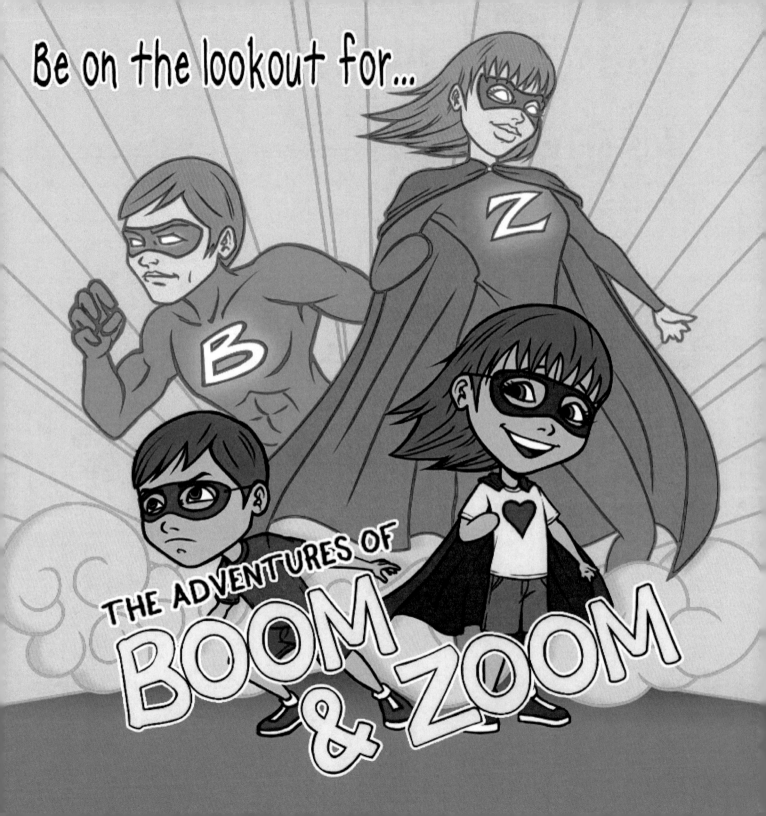

For Zoey,

Continue to spread sunshine and
happiness everywhere you go.

Published by ZoCa, LLC

ISBN 978-1-7360830-0-0

Made in United States
North Haven, CT
05 May 2022

18914718R00018